KISSED BY A ROSE

The Story of My Personal Encounters
with Saint Therese of Lisieux

ANGELA BLANCHET

Balboa Press books may be ordered through booksellers or by contacting:

Balboa Press
A Division of Hay House
1663 Liberty Drive
Bloomington, IN 47403
www.balboapress.com
1 (877) 407-4847

Because of the dynamic nature of the Internet, any web addresses or links contained in this book may have changed since publication and may no longer be valid. The views expressed in this work are solely those of the author and do not necessarily reflect the views of the publisher, and the publisher hereby disclaims any responsibility for them.

Any people depicted in stock imagery provided by Thinkstock are models, and such images are being used for illustrative purposes only. Certain stock imagery © Thinkstock.

ISBN: 978-1-5043-7884-0 (sc)
ISBN: 978-1-5043-7885-7 (e)

Library of Congress Control Number: 2017905872

Print information available on the last page.

Balboa Press rev. date: 05/02/2017

BALBOA.
PRESS
A DIVISION OF HAY HOUSE

Dedication

With all of my love and admiration, I dedicate this book to St. Therese "The Little Flower" and to Lily Rose my "little flower". Thank you to my son Ben, who reminds me every day of St. Therese's little way. A special thank you to my husband Chris, who is by my side with love and support throughout each and every spiritual endeavor.

Table of Contents

Chapter 1 | Kissed By A Rose

It was a night I will never forget. It was as if I was taken out of this world and brought to another. In fact, that's exactly what happened. As I was getting ready for bed, my bedroom filled with light, the brightest of lights. I was no longer in my home or in my bed. I was taken somewhere. It appeared to be some type of old house and there was a woman at the front door. She smiled and nodded her head. It was as if she had been waiting for me. She was an unfamiliar woman to me, but for some reason, I trusted her. The only words she said were, "St. Therese is waiting for you". I knew to follow her. We walked past many rooms before she stopped at one particular room, opened the door and motioned for me to enter.

There she stood, about 50 feet in front of me. She was a young, beautiful woman with long, brown hair and a radiance about her that left me speechless. I wanted to approach her but I couldn't. I was frozen with emotion. The feeling of love emanating from this saint was overwhelming. I found myself weeping and repeating the phrase "I love you, I love you, I love you". I truly love her, but still today I am not sure why my love for her is so real and intense.

She called to me. I was so overcome with emotion, I still can't remember if she called to me with words or a gesture, but I knew she wanted me closer to her. I was trembling as I approached her. She embraced me and I saw her face, her human face that looked at me with the purest of love and gentlest of smiles. My tears continued, and at some point I managed to utter the question, "why am I so connected to you"? She pulled her face back and looked at me with the love of a mother. She smiled and kissed me on my left shoulder and said, "Because you've been kissed by a rose so you can heal and help others".

That was not my first visitation with St. Therese, but by far the most powerful one. For days after, my physical body was shaken by the experience, but my soul was lifted. I couldn't stop picturing her in my mind. She was human. She presented herself to me in a physical body, not a spirit form, and I was in awe of this. Before I had this encounter, I would often spend time picturing what it would feel like to be in the presence of God. I am fascinated with books and conversations with people who have had an encounter with death and remember spending time in heaven only to have come back to the physical world and write about their experiences. Most express the feeling of love to be like nothing ever before, completely overpowering and embracing. This is exactly how I felt in the presence of Saint Therese. There are really no words to describe the feeling of being surrounded by love this intense. I hold onto that feeling in my difficult days. I will never forget it and I long to feel it again. I am blessed with a wonderful family, parents and a sister who love me, two beautiful children and a devoted husband of 20 years, yet I NEVER felt love so strongly before.

My very first encounter with St. Therese, was in a dream 5 years ago, where she appeared to me but did not touch me. She asked me to visit a shrine that a family had built for her, only towns away. When I awoke from this dream, I was unsure if it was just a dream. I found it strange that St. Therese would send me a message in a dream. I was raised Catholic, I believed in saints and prayed to many of them as a child, but St. Therese was not one of them. I knew very little about her life, or what miracles she may have performed. For these reasons, I didn't rush to visit that shrine. I let it go.

As the months followed, the dream visitations became more frequent and the request became louder. It became obvious to me that these dreams would recur until I went to visit her shrine. I asked my husband if he would consider taking a ride with me and our two children. Our youngest child is a boy on the autism spectrum, who at that time was six years old. I started to feel that maybe all of this was about praying for him.

In June 2011, my family set off in search for the local St. Therese shrine. I heard from many others over the years that this shrine existed. Even my mother had gone there to pray with with her friends. I had learned that a family had built a small chapel and garden for St. Therese when a miraculous healing had occurred after praying to her. The odd thing was that no one seemed to remember the exact location of the shrine and it was not listed in the phone book or advertised. We were told the general area, but no specifics. We drove around for hours, the same few miles, in circles, stopping in local stores and restaurants asking if anyone knew of a shrine built for St. Therese. There was no helpful direction and just as we were about to give up, we stumbled upon it by chance. But then again, maybe we were lead there.

As we drove down a typical residential street, we noticed this small chapel set back on the property next to an old home. There was a man standing outside of his home, directly across the street from the shrine. I asked him what we should do as I felt awkward to just walk up someone's personal property. He reassured us that it was okay and told us that hundreds of people have come over the years to pray in this little chapel.

It was a small, old, brick chapel built in the 1940s. When we walked in the lights flickered three times. There was no denying the feeling of spirit. It was overpowering. I couldn't help but be drawn to the pictures of people who had visited there through the years. Still unsure as to why I was called there, I sat and prayed. I prayed for my family. I prayed for my children. I prayed for intercession for my son. I wanted to stay longer, but I couldn't. While I was in this chapel, I couldn't breathe. My chest felt as if it was crushing and the pain was getting difficult to endure. I didn't understand this until much later on, when I learned that St. Therese had suffered and died of tuberculosis. I was feeling her past pains.

Chapter 2 | The Request For A Shrine

Months passed by after my visit to the shrine. I had stopped giving it much thought. For all I knew, I was led there to pray and had done just that. But to my surprise, the dreams and visitations began happening again. I started to have steady dreams of St. Therese. In my dreams she would always show me or hand me a statue of herself. It was similar to a statue of her I saw in the shrine we had visited. It became clear to me that this meant she wanted me to have one of the same. I began to feel the connection to the visit to the shrine. St. Therese wanted me to have my own statue of her, so I would continue to pray to her.

One day, I was eager to speak to my husband about yet another dream visitation from St. Therese. He already knew I was having many dream visitations with her. I called him at work and he happened to be in his car driving through an unfamiliar town in New Jersey. I told him about my latest communication with St. Therese the night before and I mentioned to him that I wanted to get a statue of her to put in our backyard. It was at that very moment that he happened to be stopped at a traffic light next to a church that he has never seen before. He cut me off in conversation to tell me that he thought he was looking at a statue of St. Therese in front of a church right in that very moment, as I was asking him if we could get one of our own. The light turned green and he didn't have time to be sure that what he was seeing was real, so he drove around the block to pull closer to the church. He kept me on the phone with him as he got out of the car to confirm that he was in fact looking at a large, beautiful, gray stone statue of St. Therese of Lisieux. This was unbelievable timing and synchronicity. My husband was far from his typical work area and the timing of my call was obviously intervened by St. Therese. There was no denying her request and so, of course, my husband agreed to this idea and said he would help me look for a statue right away. We spoke about putting it in our backyard surrounded by pretty flowers. This felt good to me, like I was doing what she was asking of me. It felt like the start of a special connection with this powerful saint. But, just as we started initiating our little backyard shrine, her messages to me became louder, and much more specific. In the weeks following, specific instructions from my dreams were heard. *"The statue is to be put in the front of your home, so others can see me. There are to be roses, running water, and a place for prayer petitions."*

St. Therese wanted a shrine, a place for people to pray and ask for intercession. I wrestled with following through on this, not because I didn't want to please St. Therese, but because I couldn't help but worry about how others would respond. I decided to feel it out and called my next door neighbor, who, coincidentally, moved into her home only a few months prior. I told her of my possible plan, to build a shrine for St. Therese on the side of our front property that bordered hers. I mentioned that I would be more than happy to install a fence separating our yards, so that they could keep their privacy. Her reaction not only surprised me, but reinforced what was being asked of me. She was overcome with emotion. I heard the cracking in her voice through the phone as she began to cry. Her response was not at all what I expected. She told me that if we built it, she would be out there all the time and that a fence was not necessary. She was so touched that we were going to create this shrine and felt like, in some way, this would help her as well. This was the first moment that I started to believe that people would be receptive to our shrine, and that perhaps they were in need of it.

It wasn't difficult for me to visualize the shrine, for I was shown many times what it needed to look like. I knew it would be a leap of faith to put our time, money and home out there for others to see and visit. But the more I visualized it, the more I knew that I had full belief in what was being asked of me. I trusted that St. Therese would not be asking me to do something that wouldn't be of benefit for others. She would continue to love us and take care of us for helping her with her mission.

Chapter 3 | What is St. Therese's Mission?

Prior to the visitations I had with St. Therese, I really knew nothing about her. All I knew was that she is a saint and a lot of people pray to her. However, before I created a shrine for her, I felt the need to learn more about her life, who she was and why she is greatly loved by so many. I began researching about her life and reading countless books about her. The more I learned about her, the more I loved and admired her.

St. Therese of Lisieux lived a very short life of 24 years (January 2, 1873-September 30, 1897). Sadly, her mother died of cancer when she was only four years old and she was raised by her father and her older sisters. Two of her sisters entered the Carmelite convent and she couldn't wait to do the same. Initially, she was refused by the superior of the convent because of her age. However due to her persistence, determination and strong will, at the very young age of 15, she became a Carmelite nun. Her desire to be a saint began early on in her life. However, as a Carmelite nun she knew she would never perform great works. She never went on important missions. Instead, she performed all of her ordinary tasks with extraordinary love. She found God in every person and every deed. Her love was simple and childlike. Her way became known as "the little way". *"I told myself: God would not make me wish for something impossible and so, in spite of my littleness, I can aim at being a saint."* - St. Therese

St. Therese's mission is a simple one, to remind us that God is in everything around us, to remind us to have gratitude for all of the little blessings in our life and to encourage us to perform the ordinary tasks in our own life with great love in our hearts. *"Love proves itself with good deeds, so how am I to show my love? Great deeds are forbidden of me. The only way I can prove my love is by scattering flowers and these flowers are in every little sacrifice, every glance and word, and the doing of the least actions for love."* She became fondly remembered and loved as "The Little Flower." After she died, one of her sisters put together her writings, including three manuscripts and her poetry into a book that was later entitled "The Story of A Soul" which was published in 1898. This autobiography of St. Therese quickly became a modern spiritual classic, read by millions and continues to have a powerful impact on those who read it today. In 1925, the pope declared St. Therese sainthood after four authenticated miracles of healing occurred.

I remembered hearing stories as a child about St. Therese sending roses to people from heaven, but I never really understood this. One of her requests of me was to add roses to the shrine for her. So, what is the significance of roses and St. Therese? St. Therese loved roses and as a child would often scatter rose petals. The sight of roses comforted her as she was dying from tuberculosis in the convent. She looked forward to continuing her mission after dying to help others maintain a childlike faith with God. She promised to shower people with roses from heaven as a sign that prayers are being heard and answered. *"After my death, I will let fall a shower of roses. I will spend my heaven doing good upon earth..."* Roses have become a great symbol of St. Therese. I have since read a countless number of stories about people who have prayed to her and roses have literally appeared from out of nowhere. St. Therese spreads roses, or the scent of roses, as a reminder to never lose faith in God. I was now so excited to plant roses in her honor and begin creating the shrine.

Chapter 4 | Creating The Shrine

In May 2012, we left behind our fears and concerns about what others may think, and we began to build a small, intimate shrine on our front lawn for St. Therese with all the she requested of me. There was running water, prayer cards and of course roses. We also included a sign on our front lawn that read "all are welcome to come and pray here". Our home is in a typical, middle class, residential neighborhood consisting of ranch houses and capes with about ¼ acre of property each. Homes are relatively close to one another, our property is not secluded. I knew that people would notice and ask questions, but I also knew that is what St. Therese wanted. She wanted to be noticed and being different stands out and attracts attention. She wanted people to ask so that her story could be told.

What happened immediately after we built this shrine continues to amaze me. People began to come, one at a time and the word was spreading. Some would show up with entire families, others alone with directions in hand. To say I was surprised as to the number of people coming would be an understatement. The prayer box was filling, quickly. Even young children in the neighborhood were leaving prayer requests. There are moments I can remember looking out my window that have sent chills down my spine, moments that were obvious validations that this was exactly what St. Therese wanted.

Coincidentally, or most likely not coincidentally, the bus stop to the schools in our district is right in front of my home, and now right in front of the shrine. It didn't dawn on me as we were building the shrine that every morning children and their parents would be waiting for the bus at the same location as our shrine, and every afternoon parents would be standing in front of the shrine to pick up their children. I started to notice the impact of this when I would open my curtains in the morning, look out the window and find children sitting in the shrine with their moms and dads. I often find parents taking a few minutes to pray after they say good-bye to their kids in the morning. I even see older siblings, who wait at the bus stop in the afternoon for a younger sibling, come and sit and admire the statues and angels in the shrine. Not only are people who are waiting for their children taking an opportunity to pray, but I have observed other children who are on the bus starring out the window at the shrine in wonderment. You can tell by their innocent stares, they are intrigued. The irony of it is, that when I was asked by St. Therese to please put the statue of her in my front yard instead of my backyard, the initial side of the front property we were going to do this was on the right side. But, as we began to take initiative with our plans, St. Therese returned to me and showed me the shrine being moved to the left side of our property. I didn't understand why she wanted it there, being that the left side was much closer to the property line of my neighbor. Now, it is crystal clear to me that the reason St. Therese wanted the shrine on the left of my home is because that is where the bus stop is (and a stop sign too). It is where people stop, people wait and people gather. It is where people notice her. She couldn't have planned it any better.

Photo of our St. Therese Shrine

Additional Photo of our St. Therese Shrine

Evening In The Shrine

Chapter 5 | Passers By

There is a young man in our neighborhood who runs every day. He is in his 20s, athletic build and has been running past our home for years. Shortly after we built the shrine, I happened to look out the window one day, at the exact moment he was running past my home. He looked at the shrine, kept his running pace and blessed himself with the sign of the cross. Wow. I was so taken back by this moment, partly because I was allowing myself to judge a book by its cover. For some irrational reason, this young man did not "look" to be prayerful or spiritual. I felt silly that, for a second, I would even think such a thing. Of course there is no specific look to a person connected to their faith. In this moment, I began to realize that the prayer shrine I had built for others to come and pray was also indirectly teaching me about faith and God. I welcomed these lessons and I knew there were many more to come.

This was not the only time that I looked out the window at the exact moment someone was walking past the shrine and blessing themselves. I am fascinated by the intricate timing of these moments. What is the probability that in the exact second I decide to look out my window someone is looking at St. Therese and the shrine around her and making the sign of the cross? Obviously, somehow, I am being nudged to do so, because it reaffirms that she is being noticed and that people are comforted by this. In my neighborhood, it is common for residents to hire landscapers to mow their lawns in the summer. Four times this past summer, I looked out the window and saw a young man riding on a mower from one of my neighbor's homes, past my house, to another neighbor. On all four occasions, the exact moments I have noticed him were the exact moments he was blessing himself, by taking out a cross he wears around his neck, looking at Saint Therese and kissing his necklace, all while in motion on the mower. I can't get enough of these moments. I know that St. Therese is behind the timing that allows me to see them and I'm so grateful for that.

I watched as the UPS delivery truck slowed down in front of my home one day. The only thought I had was a wonderment as to what it was I was receiving. I was trying to remember if I ordered something or maybe someone bought me a gift? I waited impatiently for the man to get out of his truck, but he didn't. What was taking him so long? Maybe it was a large delivery and he needed time? After several minutes passed, I realized no package was being delivered. This man had pulled over in his truck to pray. He parked the truck in front of the shrine and never came out. He sat in prayer for a few minutes and drove away. I was humbled by this experience and realized that was a much better gift than any delivery could have been.

Recently, on my way out to run errands with my children, I was startled to see a police car parked in front of my home, directly in front of the prayer shrine. This made me anxious and I immediately wondered what type of legal trouble we could be in from creating the shrine. It seemed as if the officer had his head down filling out paperwork. He would look out his window at the shrine and then hang his head down in a way that made him appear to be writing. To my surprise, once again, as I looked more carefully, it became obvious that he officer had his head down in prayer. He was taking time out in his day, a few minutes, to connect to his faith in prayer. These are such powerful moments and amazing reminders that we are all seeking peace and comfort.

Usually, when I look out my window and find someone sitting and praying in the shrine, I keep my distance and give them their privacy. Occasionally, however, I am pulled toward going out to greet them. One summer day, shortly after we built the shrine, this was the case. I noticed a woman praying in front of the St. Therese statue. I was drawn to her. She had rosary beads around her neck and a warm smile that spoke volumes to me. I already knew there would be more to our meeting than a one- time visit. She asked me questions about why I made a shrine for St. Therese. We chatted for a few minutes and then she asked me if she could give me something. She walked me to her car and opened the trunk. The back of her car reminded me of the car of a salesperson, packed with boxes of items that they may be selling door to door. But, in this case, it was different. This woman wasn't selling anything. She was giving…prayer cards, prayer metals, saint items, rosary beads, religious books, even some statues. She asked me what I wanted for the shrine so I can give to those who come. I have learned over the years to receive graciously knowing that this giving would come back to her ten-fold. I admired the Mother Mary ring on her finger, which she then removed and placed onto mine. I was completely taken back. For months following, there were many times that I would come home to find a box sitting on my front steps. They were "refills" from this amazing woman. I learned from meeting her that God is working through many people in different ways, but with the same mission that Saint Therese teaches us, to spread love and good deeds in any little way we can. When you find yourself on that mission, giving with all of your heart and self, you then become fortunate enough to meet others who are doing the same.

"Without love, deeds, even the most brilliant, count as nothing." – *St. Therese*

Chapter 6 | Flowers At The Shrine

Keeping the shrine filled with flowers is something that is very important to me, especially since St. Therese is known as "the little flower". However, I found it difficult to keep up with always having flowers in bloom out in the shrine. On two different occasions, two different people mentioned to me that funeral parlors often give away baskets of flowers to local hospitals and foundations after services are completed. I have learned that when you are receiving a message from God, the angels, saints, etc. and you don't respond to it the first time, they repeat themselves so that you give it a second thought. They nudge you harder to take action. So, I decided to make a call to a local funeral home. I explained to the owner that I have a shrine for St. Therese which I love to keep filled with fresh flowers because people come often to pray. She was thrilled to hear from me and immediately told me that St. Therese holds a special place in her heart. Apparently, her husband had significant medical ailments and her family is very devoted to Saint Therese. Without getting into much detail, she mentioned receiving many miracles from St. Therese after praying her novena. At this point, I knew that St. Therese had set up this connection. It's now four years later, and we continue to receive calls from them to come pick up beautiful bouquets and baskets of flowers. When vases of roses are available, they always think of St. Therese. The most interesting part of all of this is the timing of when I receive a call. The phone call to let us know they have flowers available to us always seems to come when I need reassurance from St. Therese.

My son, Ben, who is on the autism spectrum, also has significant medical challenges. It didn't take me long to notice that every time he has an important doctor appointment or procedure,

I would receive a call that there are flowers for the shrine. One day, Ben was having a more complicated procedure and I was doing my best not to worry. The phone rang, my husband answered it and then told me he was on the way to the funeral home to pick up flowers. I wasn't surprised. However, after he came home and unloaded tons of flowers, he said he needed to go back to pick up more. There were so many flowers, he couldn't fit them all into his car the first time. It never ceases to amaze me how St. Therese lines up people, places and circumstances to remind us of her presence and to help us keep the faith.

Chapter 7 | A Visit From Archangel Michael

After the creation of the shrine, as fall neared, I realized that October 1st is the feast day of St. Therese and I knew that feast days are often celebrated. Feast days are a special day set aside to remember certain individuals with special mentions and prayers. I thought having a feast day celebration would be a great way to honor St. Therese and continue to spread the word about the shrine. So, we began to plan one. I told my family about the date, Sunday, September 30th (2012). Shortly after, I received an interesting phone call from my sister. I could tell by her "hello" that she had been anxiously waiting to talk to me all morning, but waited for a decent hour to call. She eagerly told me, "I had a dream last night about Archangel Michael and I know that I have to share it with you". My sister has had encounters with angels for years, so I wasn't too surprised to hear her say this, but I was of course quite intrigued. She told me that Archangel Michael (Saint Michael) visited her in her dream and made an adamant statement, "Tell your sister that I want to be in her shrine". She told me she knew that she had to share this message with me right away because in the dream St. Michael was very loud and very clear and kept repeating the phrase "Are you listening to me"? Without a second thought, I got off the phone and immediately onto my computer to research a company with which to place an order for a beautiful Archangel Michael statue.

I started to reflect upon my sister's dream. I thought maybe St. Michael wanted to be here for the feast day celebration, so when I placed my order over the phone, I asked the gentleman who was assisting me, how long it would take to be delivered. He told me that the statue ships from Italy and would take about six weeks and there would, unfortunately, be no way that the statue would arrive by September 30th. As days past, and it was closer to the end of September, I received a call from a good friend who asked me if I wanted to attend the St. Michael Feast Day celebration on Saturday the 29th at a local church. I immediately found this to be a crazy coincidence. Was St. Michael's feast day that close to the feast day of St. Therese? Of course, I looked into it right away and sure enough St. Michael's feast day is September 29th. I became more and more convinced that the St. Michael statue would arrive early to my home. Originally, I thought that St. Michael asked to be put in the St. Therese shrine in order to be a part of HER feast day, but little did I know it was the same timing as HIS feast day. This was all very synchronistic. I became increasingly curious if the statue would arrive in time for HIS day and on September 29^{th,} I called the company to check on the order. I received the company voicemail, so I left a message with my name and order number and asked for someone to please call me back with the status of my order. I remember hanging up the phone, looking up to the sky and saying "Archangel Michael you have wings and you have power. If you want to be here for your day, then I know you can." Part of me was joking, but part of me wasn't, because I sensed a bigger picture to all of this. About an hour later, UPS showed up at my front door with a delivery. The box was so big, I immediately knew what it was. St. Michael was here, with time to spare! I opened the box outside and immediately placed him in the shrine. The statue was beautiful! I took pictures and texted them to my sister with a message saying, "Look who got himself here on time". I then went inside to answer my home phone that I could hear ringing from outside. It was a man, named Michael (of all names), calling me back from the company with whom I ordered the statue. I said, "Hi Michael, I am so sorry to have bothered you and wasted your time with my message. My delivery just arrived. The statue of Archangel Michael is beautiful and I am very grateful." He replied, "What are you talking about? That's not possible! I called to tell you that the St. Michael statue is backordered and will take an extra few weeks to be delivered. You may not have it for a month or so." I responded, "But I already have it. I opened the box and he is here." He then replied quite confused, "Look lady, I don't know what type of magic you are working there, but I don't think that statue came from us." I immediately ran outside to the opened box I had thrown in the garbage and realized there was no return address on the box and no packing slip. There was no indication of where the statue came from. But I knew where it came from. It came from Archangel Michael's strong desire to be included in the shrine, to be present on his feast day and on the feast day of St. Therese when many people would come to pray. He wanted to be visible to others alongside of her. As much as this shrine is for St. Therese to help carry on her missions, that was the moment I realized that they are all working together…..God, Jesus, all the angels and saints. They all want the same for us. They want us to open our hearts to prayer, connection, trust and faith, and if we do so, we may just find a small miracle waiting for us.

Similar to the way in which Archangel Michael brought himself to the shrine, St. Therese chose a special bench for the shrine. A very close friend of mine, who lost her brother recently, donated money to the St. Therese shrine in his name. At this time, the shrine really needed a new bench. I shopped carefully and was excited to choose one. I found one online that I really liked and placed the order for it. When the bench arrived, I was very surprised to see it wasn't the bench I ordered. However, it was even nicer than the one I had chosen. I logged into the website to review that order, and somehow, someway, a completely different bench order had been placed. I laughed as I realized St. Therese chose her own bench! I don't for one second doubt that we are working together and when she wants something to be a certain way, she sure can make it happen!

Chapter 8 | Meeting A Special Needs Child At The Shrine

As a mother of a young boy with autism, I have had the honor of meeting and bonding with other mothers over the years that are also parenting a child on the spectrum. I know first-hand how special and pure of heart these children really are. Their innocence carries throughout their lives and sometimes I feel that their unawareness of the world around them can be a blessing in disguise. My son, Ben, who is now 11 years old, still does not recognize embarrassment or shame, hatefulness or revenge. He knows love in its purest form. He talks about God in his own way and speaks of St. Therese as "the little flower who sits in the shrine to protect everyone." When I built the shrine, I knew instinctively that many families with special needs children would come to pray, or at least I hoped so.

His name was Andrew, and I don't think I will ever forget his reaction to the holy items that I gave him. One day, Andrew and his mom came to pray in the shrine. At the time, Andrew was a 14 year old boy with autism. His mom brought me to tears as she shared with me the story of having to bring him to a home when he was younger. She told me she gave him to God and prayed to Mary on her knees to take care of him and bring him back to her one day. She made a promise to God in return that she would forever carry on the work of helping others. Her prayers were answered as Andrew made incredible progress. To me, Andrew seemed like a high functioning boy on the spectrum. But, when his mother described in great detail what his behaviors and level of functioning were like prior to bringing him to a residential school, I was in shock and awe of his improvement. What stood out to me the most, was the happiness on this boy's face when I handed him a saint medal. Because of his joyful expression, I asked

Andrew if he wanted to look through my boxes of religious gifts that I offer people when they come to the shrine. He jumped at the chance, and with all of his heart he admired every medal, every prayer card, every rosary and every statue. With each new item he held, he said with such pride, "mom look at this" and "mom look at that". That day I handed over a whole box of religious gifts to Andrew and he was beaming from ear to ear. He couldn't wait to go home to show his grandma. A few days later, his mom called to tell me that he had brought some of the medals and statues to school with him. Andrew reminded me so much of my son and many other children I know who have special needs. Maybe these children will never understand the words of the "Our Father" or "Hail Mary", or maybe they won't be able to sit through an entire mass, but the purity of their souls connects them to God in their own "little way". I will always be grateful for meeting Andrew who, still to this day, reminds me of St. Therese's child-like faith.

"Each prayer is more beautiful than the others. I cannot recite them all and not knowing which to choose, I do like children who do not know how to read, I say very simply to God what I wish to say, without composing beautiful sentences, and he always understands me. For me, prayer is an aspiration of the heart, it is a simple glance directed to heaven, it is something great, supernatural, which expands my soul and unites me to Jesus." – St. Therese

Chapter 9 | Saint Therese Wants To Be Seen

I had received a call one day about an autism documentary that was being filmed by an independent film maker who has a son with autism. It was a documentary about music and art and children with special needs. Because my son Ben is on the spectrum and is musically gifted, he was asked to be included in this film. We were so excited, as we love to be involved with autism awareness. Over the years, my husband and I have organized many autism fundraisers. We often have them on our front lawn in order to include the St. Therese shrine. I know she helps us with our autism awareness projects as we help to share her story and her mission.

It was May, and most of the roses in the shrine had yet to bloom. We were preparing for the film maker to come to our home. I was really eager for our family to be involved with what I felt to be a very important autism documentary. I went outside to put mail in our mailbox and I heard the neighbor across the street yell out to me, "How did you get your roses to bloom so beautifully, mine aren't even close to coming up?" What? Last I noticed, a few days prior, was that we had yet to see roses bloom in the prayer garden. I glanced over at the shrine and lo and behold, the roses on the trellis around the Saint Therese statue were opened and gorgeous! The colors were vibrant and alive. That particular day, with no extra effort on our part, the shrine looked picture perfect. It was as if St. Therese was getting herself ready to be seen.

The man had driven two hours to come to our home. When he arrived, I immediately noticed how warm and kind natured he was. As I was helping him carry things from his car, we walked across my front lawn and he, of course, noticed the St. Therese shrine. He instantly began asking me questions about it. He was quite intrigued and the first thing he told me was that his mom would absolutely love the shrine. I knew that we had to focus on getting Ben filmed and discussing autism and music, so I spoke to him briefly about the shrine and then began discussing the film. As he was getting his camera ready, he asked me if I wouldn't mind talking off camera, in more detail, about the shrine and why it was there. I was more than happy to talk about it. I would graciously talk about Saint Therese any day or time. I was just surprised how much HE wanted to discuss it, being that it was not the reason he came to our home. The more I opened up about the story behind the shrine, the more interested he became.

After filming the footage for his documentary, the man asked me if he could keep his camera rolling. He wanted to film me telling the story about the St. Therese shrine while walking with him through the prayer garden. It was at this moment that I realized why St. Therese's roses perfectly bloomed that day. She knew this was going to happen. I was certain that she orchestrated it herself. A few weeks later, I received an email with an attachment of an amazing video presentation of our St. Therese shrine from this very open and spiritual man. He didn't ask for money or for anything in return. He simply wanted to help share our story so that others may see it and become inspired to visit. I have always found synchronicity between anything we do for autism and signs from St. Therese. On this occasion, it was undeniable!

Chapter 10 | Saint Therese Coincidences

Since my connection with St. Therese began, I have created many types of flyers and literature about her, including a banner with her photos that we hang for our feast day celebrations. I become very particular about wanting to use actual photographs that were taken of her throughout her life and not portraits painted of her. I feel so incredibly blessed to have had visitations from Saint Therese and I feel like the portraits drawn of her do not do her justice. To me, they minimize her beauty and her youthfulness. Below is the photograph that I feel best depicts her humanness and grace. It is the closest to the visions that I have seen of her.

My Favorite Photo of St. Therese

On many different occasions over the last few years, people who know my family and see a photograph of St. Therese as a child, comment about the resemblance between her and my daughter, Lily. My daughter's name is Lily Rose. I have been calling her my "little flower" years before I had any encounters with Saint Therese or any knowledge that she too is referred to as the "little flower". This cannot be a coincidence. There are obvious signs that St. Therese was connecting with me long before I had any awareness of her. As I look back, I recognize another St. Therese "coincidence" in my life. St. Therese's birthday is January 2nd. January 2nd is also the date I met my husband of 20 years. She has been bringing love and miracles into my life long before I knew her.

Every January 2nd, on her birthday, I always receive a rose from St. Therese. I either see or smell one. However, on one particular January 2nd a few years ago, I began to wonder where she was because my sign didn't come until later that evening. I remember on this day praying extra hard to Saint Therese for a sign that she is with me, that she hears my prayers and that she is pleased with all of my efforts. Also at this time, my son was having medical issues and I prayed for her to show me that she is helping him as well. I waited and waited for my rose, her signature that lets me know she is near. However, evening came and I still saw nothing. I thought to myself that this is so unlike St. Therese. Whenever I pray or call to her she always makes it so obvious for me that she is with me. I always get my rose! I tried not to doubt this connection, but it was getting closer to bedtime and I started to feel disappointment, as I thought maybe this time she was unaware of me. It was at this point that my friend, who is also my next door neighbor, sent me a text message. I had texted her earlier that evening just to say hello. Apparently, my text came to her phone as she was watching television and a particular commercial was on that made her think of me. Knowing my connection to St. Therese and how I am always planting roses around the shrine, she couldn't believe the timing of what she was hearing, so she paused the television, rewound the commercial, recorded it and sent it to me as a text audio. When I played it, this is what I heard, "No one says to stop and feel, or taste, or touch the roses. They say to stop and smell the roses." I was so amazed and relieved that at the end of a day of waiting for my roses from St. Therese, I opened up a text message and heard this. It shouldn't have surprised me, she never lets me down. What I learned that day is to never doubt that we are being guided and protected by these heavenly intercessors. We are always being heard, and if we expect to hear back from them, we will.

Since the awareness of my connection with St. Therese has grown over the years, I have also noticed others being aware of her presence. Recently, a close friend of mine was in a car accident that could have easily resulted in more serious injuries than it did. Her vehicle was hit while turning at a major intersection and her car spun into a multiple vehicle accident. She told me that the emergency responders commented that they were surprised she was as alert as she was. She was taken by ambulance to the hospital. While in the emergency room, she took off her jacket and out fell a medal of St. Therese that she had received at our feast day celebration months prior. She wondered if this meant St. Therese had protected her. She may have wondered, but I was certain of it. I know that when you carry her with you, she carries you through.

I find the kindest people visit our shrine who themselves have some amazing stories about their own connections to St. Therese. A woman visiting the shrine once shared with me that her husband was very connected to St. Therese and prayed to her often. Years ago, her family faced a great scare when her son was ill and in a comma. Her husband prayed hard to Saint Therese. Thankfully, this boy made it out of his comma and later told his mom that it was St. Therese who "tapped him on the shoulder" to wake him up. She said it wasn't his time to stay there and he was needed to go back. What an amazing validation of her powerful intercessions!

Another woman shared with me her special sign from St. Therese. She was only 19 years old when her mom died. Looking for comfort, she then began a close connection with St. Therese. She prayed to her often and read her autobiography, "Story of A Soul". As a young woman, she moved from New Jersey to Washington D.C. She got a job, her own apartment and began to live independently. Soon after she moved, she met a man and began dating, but didn't want to get serious too quickly or take the relationship too far. She wanted to stay true to her values, but this caused arguments in the relationship. One day, while in the middle of praying a St. Therese novena to help her gain clarity on how to handle this relationship, her boyfriend came knocking furiously at her door. Her instinct was not to open the door. She stayed in her apartment and he stayed outside for some time before he finally left. She went into her bedroom and prayed for St. Therese to please send her a rose! She was looking for validation to stay true to herself. The next morning, she opened her front door to get the newspaper and a rose fell from the very tiny rim on the top of the door! Wow! This amazing saint can literally make a rose appear out of nowhere. For her, it was an important confirmation that St. Therese is always by her side.

I continue to hear about prayers answered after saying a novena to St. Therese. Another heartwarming story was recently shared with me by a woman who had difficulty conceiving her children. After experiencing heartbreak from her first marriage, she would pray diligently for comfort from St. Therese. She rekindled a relationship with a previous boyfriend. As time went on in this relationship, he confided in her that it would be difficult for them to conceive children, due to an accident he had when he was quite young. This seemed irrelevant to her as they fell in love and married two years later. She worked a desk job and everyday around 7:30 am she would sit at her desk and start her day by saying a novena to St. Therese. She began to ask for a sign that they would be able to conceive and become parents. A few weeks later, she thought she had the flu as she was feeling dizzy and sick to her stomach. She began that day with her St. Therese novena and around 9am received a phone message with a name that took her by surprise. The woman who left a message had the name "Teresa Rose". She immediately took this as a sign that her prayers were being answered. This prompted her to take a pregnancy test during lunch. To her amazement, it was positive and she was blessed with a son eight months later.

Chapter 11 | Writing The Book

Initially, when I began writing about my encounters with St. Therese, it wasn't a book I was writing. I wanted to have a simple brochure or handout to give to those who visited the shrine that explains the story of why we created it. However, as I began to write I started having dreams where St. Therese handed me the writing in a book. It made sense to me, since I know that St. Therese is all about spreading her word and her mission. Obviously, there would be more readers of a book than a local handout. So I began to write. I wrote a little and then put the book away and before I knew it, a few years had passed. Life got busy with caring for my children, working etc. Time went on and I got a new computer. Then one day, the dreams came back and St. Therese began handing me the book again. I knew I needed to finish it. I went onto my computer forgetting that at this point, I had a whole new computer system. I searched files and old emails to try to find my earlier writing, but it was gone. I was so disappointed. I had no writing in hand, but the dreams were closer together and persistent. She wants a book. Did I need to start writing all over again? I started to talk to her and asked her for a sign. Within the next few weeks, I received so many signs that St. Therese was around me. A friend dropped off a little statue of St. Therese with a note saying "thinking of you", another friend sent me an email that contained only a single picture of a rose with the same message "thinking of you". More people were coming to the shrine asking me about St. Therese and her birthday, January 2nd, was approaching. I had a feeling she would give me the biggest sign on her birthday, and she did just that. On January 2nd, I went into an old file draw to dig out some tax paperwork, and there it was neatly stapled together…..the book I had begun writing for her, three years prior! I then knew I had to make finishing the book a priority and I was excited to do so.

One night, I was sitting at my computer working on the book, reading about St. Therese and scrolling through images of her. I wanted this time to be quiet time, so I could keep focused and be productive. I heard a text message alert come to my phone and my first thought was an annoyed one because I really didn't want to be interrupted. It was from my mother's friend's daughter, who I know from over the years, but only hear from occasionally. The timing of her text was uncanny and I had the chills from head to toe as I read it. "Hi Angela, an interesting thing happened to me. I was back in my elementary school the other day and as I was walking around my old school, I noticed that they built a chapel downstairs that is dedicated to St. Therese of Lisieux (The Little Flower). There was a big picture of her outside on the wall. As soon as I looked at the picture, I noticed that she has a very strong energy. I didn't even want to look at her picture directly in the eyes, the energy was super intense. I started getting energy rushes while standing there reading the plaque on the wall about her. Then I was telling my mom about her and she mentioned that you have a shrine of her in your yard and that you also found her energy to be very powerful. I don't know much about her, but now I'm researching because of this experience." I kept starring at this message and starring at all of the Saint Therese pictures and writing I had out on the table at the same time. Talk about timing! I took pictures of what my surroundings looked like at that moment and sent a message back to this woman saying, "This is what I was doing when you sent this message to me." Then I picked up the phone to call her. We spoke for a while about the synchronistic timing of our thoughts. She asked me questions about Saint Therese and seemed very eager to learn more about her. This was an obvious sign for her to do so, and a definite sign for me that writing this book will encourage others to want to read and learn more about St. Therese, which has been her divine plan all along.

As I was nearing the end of writing this book, I went to sleep one night pondering on the best way to end the book. That evening, I was lucky enough to have a quick visitation from this powerful Saint and although I don't remember all that she told me, I do remember this. I saw her face, just her face. It was her profile, actually. She had a gentile smile and said *"There are more colors here than colors in the crayons. There is more love here than all the love on earth. There is more credence when we work together."* I reflected on this as soon as I woke up and continued to hold onto these words all day. I don't believe that she was speaking just to me. I believe that this message is for us all. She is telling us about the beauty of heaven, referring to colors we have all yet to see. She is reminding us that there is a love stronger than any love we have ever felt here and she is asking us to all work together because when we do, we help others to restore their belief and their faith in God's love for them bringing healing, peace and comfort to one another.

"To live in love is to sail forever, spreading seeds of joy and peace in hearts."- St. Therese

To this day, I still don't really understand why St. Therese has appeared to me. Maybe it was because my energy is open to receiving messages? Maybe it's because she knew I would follow through? I guess I will never really know. However, what I do know is that I feel honored and privileged to have received her. What I do know is that through our interactions, I have become even more faithful and so very inspired. St. Therese will always be an inspiration for me. When I have a challenging day, I remember how she lived her life, never taking anything for granted, always putting out love and kindness even when others weren't treating her the same. She was a brave, spirited young woman whose autobiography impacted so many after she died. I think of her with every little good deed I do. I feel her presence and desire for others to learn about her so she can shower them with roses from heaven. My hope is that after reading this book, you consider carrying on her mission of performing your ordinary tasks in your life with extraordinary love in your heart.

CPSIA information can be obtained
at www.ICGtesting.com
Printed in the USA
BVOW05s2159250517

485250BV00003B/4/P